XTREME ARMED FORCES

GREEN BERETS

A&D Xtreme
BOLD HI-LO NONFICTION
An imprint of Abdo Publishing
abdobooks.com

JOHN HAMILTON

TAKE IT TO
THE XTREME!

GET READY FOR AN XTREME ADVENTURE!
THE PAGES OF THIS BOOK WILL TAKE YOU INTO THE THRILLING
WORLD OF THE UNITED STATES GREEN BERETS.
WHEN YOU HAVE FINISHED READING THIS BOOK, TAKE THE
XTREME CHALLENGE ON PAGE 45 ABOUT WHAT YOU'VE LEARNED!

ABDOBOOKS.COM

Published by Abdo Publishing, a division of ABDO, PO Box 398166, Minneapolis, Minnesota 55439. Copyright © 2021 by Abdo Consulting Group, Inc. International copyrights reserved in all countries. No part of this book may be reproduced in any form without written permission from the publisher. A&D Xtreme™ is a trademark and logo of Abdo Publishing.

Printed in the United States of America, North Mankato, MN.

102020

012021

THIS BOOK CONTAINS
RECYCLED MATERIALS

Editor: Sue Hamilton; Copy Editor: Bridget O'Brien

Graphic Design: Sue Hamilton; Imprint Template Design: Dorothy Toth

Cover Design: Laura Graphenteen

Cover Photo: US Air Force

Interior Photos & Illustrations: All images US Army except: Alamy-pgs 12-13; CIA-pgs 8 & 9; National Archives-pg 15 (inset); US Air Force-pgs 34-35; US Marine Corps-pgs 26-27; US National Guard-pgs 24-25.

LIBRARY OF CONGRESS CONTROL NUMBER: 2020940448

PUBLISHER'S CATALOGING-IN-PUBLICATION DATA

Names: Hamilton, John, author.

Title: Green Berets / by John Hamilton

Description: Minneapolis, Minnesota : Abdo Publishing, 2021 | Series: Xtreme armed forces | Includes online resources and index

Identifiers: ISBN 9781532194559 (lib. bdg.) | ISBN 9781098213985 (ebook)

Subjects: LCSH: United States. Army. Special Forces--Juvenile literature. | United States--Armed Forces--Juvenile literature. | Special forces (Military science)--Juvenile literature. | Military departments and divisions--Juvenile literature.

Classification: DDC 356.16--dc23

TABLE OF
CONTENTS

CHAPTER 1

GREEN BERETS

Green Beret soldiers exchange fire
with enemy fighters who attacked
US allied bases in Afghanistan.

The United States Army's Special Forces troops, commonly called the Green Berets, are some of the best-trained fighters in the US military. They are a special operations force that works in small teams. They carry out missions quickly and secretly.

When dangerous, top-secret missions are required, the Army's Special Forces are among the first to be sent in. They can operate in small groups inside foreign lands for long stretches of time.

XTREME FACT

The Green Berets' motto is the Latin phrase *De Oppresso Liber*. It means, "To Liberate the Oppressed."

The Green Berets are both warriors and US ambassadors. One of their main missions is to train foreign **allied** military forces.

Green Berets training in Syria.

CHAPTER 2

GREEN BERETS
HISTORY

The Green Berets can trace their roots to the US Office of Strategic Services (OSS). The OSS was an intelligence agency formed during World War II. Many of its **guerrilla fighters** were from the US Army. They gathered information, ambushed the enemy, and trained local resistance fighters.

General William "Wild Bill" Donovan (seated center) was head of the OSS during World War II.

During World War II, OSS Detachment 101 troops parachuted behind Japanese lines in Burma. They attacked Japanese bases, called in allied air strikes, and rescued hundreds of downed allied pilots.

Members of an OSS team prepare to parachute behind enemy lines during World War II.

In 1952, the first Army Special Forces group was formed. Its mission was to conduct **guerrilla warfare** and train foreign armies to fight the enemies of the United States. The group was led by Colonel Aaron Bank, known today as the father of the Special Forces.

Colonel Bank (second from left) observes Army Special Forces prone pistol training.

XTREME FACT

Colonel Bank was an OSS officer during World War II. He secretly parachuted into France and organized guerrilla warfare against Germany.

The Green Berets were very active in Southeast Asia during the Vietnam War. Later, they disrupted drug traffickers in Colombia and other South and Central American countries.

Green Berets train South Vietnamese soldiers in 1964.

Green Berets fought during the invasion of Panama in 1989. They have also fought in Iraq and Afghanistan during the **War on Terror**.

CHAPTER 3

HEADGEAR

In 1954, Army Special Forces troops adopted a unique, dark-green headgear. It set them apart from troops in the regular Army. It also gave them their nickname: the Green Berets. The headgear was based on berets worn by elite British **commandos**.

XTREME FACT

President Kennedy said the green berets worn by Special Forces soldiers were a "symbol of excellence, a badge of courage, a mark of distinction in the fight for freedom."

President John F. Kennedy made the berets an official part of Army Special Forces' uniform in 1962.

CHAPTER 4

TRAINING

After a screening process, Green Beret candidates begin the Special Forces Qualification Course, also known as the Q Course. It lasts about 53 weeks. Candidates undergo extreme physical conditioning. They learn advanced combat skills. Intelligence and resourcefulness are also required.

Trainees use a log for building teamwork.

A Green Beret team trains in building assault and entry.

During training, candidates learn how to survive in enemy territory. They learn to work together in squads. They learn advanced marksmanship skills, how to use explosives, and how to parachute from high altitudes. They also master foreign languages in order to train forces in foreign countries.

XTREME FACT

After graduating from Q Course, Green Berets continue training for many weeks. They learn advanced skills such as hostage rescue, cold-weather survival, and mountaineering.

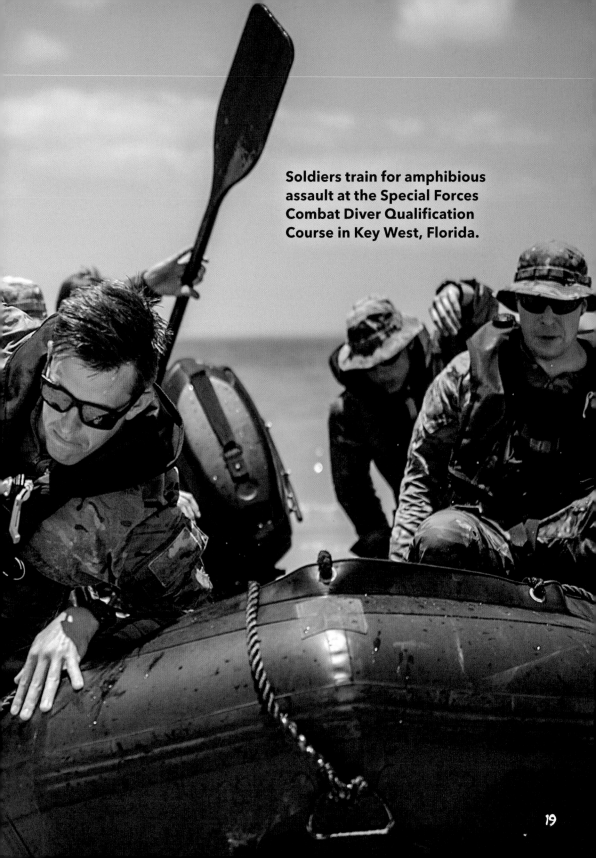

Soldiers train for amphibious assault at the Special Forces Combat Diver Qualification Course in Key West, Florida.

CHAPTER 5

WEAPONS &
EQUIPMENT

Special Forces soldiers are trained to use almost any kind of weapon, from pistols to rocket launchers. They often carry short-barreled rifles called carbines. These weapons make it easier to move in small spaces, such as through doorways. Green Berets often carry M4A1 carbine or MK 17 SCAR-H **assault rifles**.

XTREME FACT

Both the M4A1 and MK 17 SCAR-H can be fitted with a grenade launcher under the barrel.

A Green Beret uses a M4A1 carbine assault rifle on a practice range that mimics combat actions.

Depending on their mission, Green Beret soldiers use a variety of special gear. Equipment might include GPS locators, satellite communications gear, scuba gear, or night vision goggles. Rebreathers are special underwater breathing devices. They let Special Forces soldiers swim hidden underwater in enemy territory without producing telltale bubbles.

A Special Forces soldier swims with a rebreather during combat dive training.

Night vision goggles allow soldiers to see in the dark, as well as in smoky or dusty areas.

CHAPTER 6

SURVIVAL SKILLS

The Green Berets are trained to fight and survive in any environment. They can travel to their targets by air, land, or sea. They can survive off the land for weeks at a time, whether they are in forests, steamy jungles, deserts, mountains, or even frozen Arctic areas.

A soldier parachutes into a mountainous area of Washington state.

CHAPTER 7

A-TEAMS

The Green Berets are organized into small groups called A-Teams. That is short for Operational Detachment-Alphas.

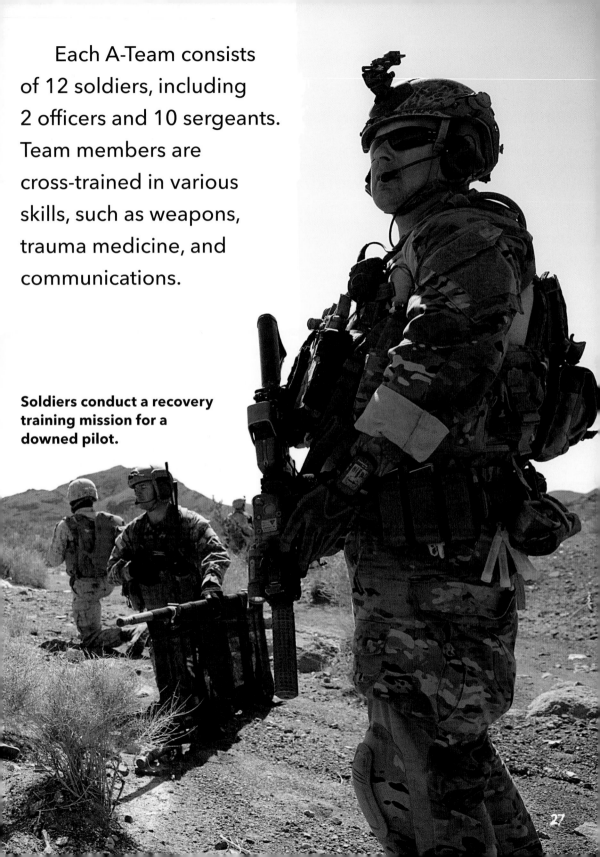

Each A-Team consists of 12 soldiers, including 2 officers and 10 sergeants. Team members are cross-trained in various skills, such as weapons, trauma medicine, and communications.

Soldiers conduct a recovery training mission for a downed pilot.

A-Team members rely on **stealth** to carry out their missions. They speak foreign languages. They can operate in hostile areas for long periods of time without help or supervision. Their training prepares them for the stresses they will experience working behind enemy lines.

US Special Forces work with an Afghanistan commando to rescue a soldier in enemy territory.

CHAPTER 8

RECONNAISSANCE

A Green Beret studies
a map discovered
during a reconnaissance
training mission.

Before US armed forces attack a country, much must first be known about the enemy. An important job of the Army Special Forces is reconnaissance. Green Berets sneak undetected behind enemy lines. They gather as much information as possible, including the opponent's troop strength, movement, and weapons.

Green Berets practice a Special Purpose Insertion Extraction (SPIES). SPIES are used when soldiers are in areas that do not allow helicopters to land.

After gathering details about the enemy, Special Forces soldiers use satellite radios to send information back to their commanders. The data helps US forces prepare for more effective attacks, which saves lives. When their reconnaissance mission is complete, Green Beret teams are quickly **exfiltrated** out of enemy territory, often by helicopter.

XTREME FACT

Army Special Forces were sent to Afghanistan weeks before the US invasion in October 2001. Their covert reconnaissance helped topple the Taliban and al-Qaeda terrorist networks.

CHAPTER 9

TRAINING

FOREIGN TROOPS

A Green Beret trains members of Colombia's air force.

One of the most important missions carried out by Special Forces is "foreign internal defense." This means training foreign troops to fight enemy forces. The Green Berets teach and organize foreign soldiers to defend their homeland as well as fight the enemies of the United States.

XTREME FACT

During the Cold War, the Green Berets helped foreign armies fight Communist aggressors. Today, the Green Berets assist many countries, including Colombia and Afghanistan, to fight drug traffickers and insurgents.

Green Beret soldiers train foreign **allies** to battle **insurgent forces**. These counterinsurgency missions stabilize friendly governments. It prevents them from

Honduran commandos are taught camouflage skills by Green Beret soldiers to help in their fight against drug trafficking.

falling into the hands of new leaders who might be hostile to the United States. Green Berets also supply friendly forces with effective weapons and equipment.

CHAPTER 10

DIRECT ACTION

Direct action missions are strikes against the enemy. They are short duration. That means they do not last long, like regular military actions. The Green Berets use the element of surprise to perform lightning-fast missions. They include attacking enemy troops, destroying equipment, blowing up bridges, disrupting communications, or rescuing soldiers.

Firebombs are set off in an Iraqi palm grove to destroy hidden enemy weapons and explosives.

CHAPTER 11

COUNTERTERRORISM

One of the missions of the Army Special Forces is to fight **terrorists** in foreign lands. The Green Berets are specially trained in hostage rescue and advanced combat techniques. That includes fast roping into dangerous enemy areas to strike terrorists. This method allows for soldiers to quickly exit a hovering helicopter by sliding down a rope to the ground or a building rooftop.

A Green Beret fast ropes from a helicopter to the ground.

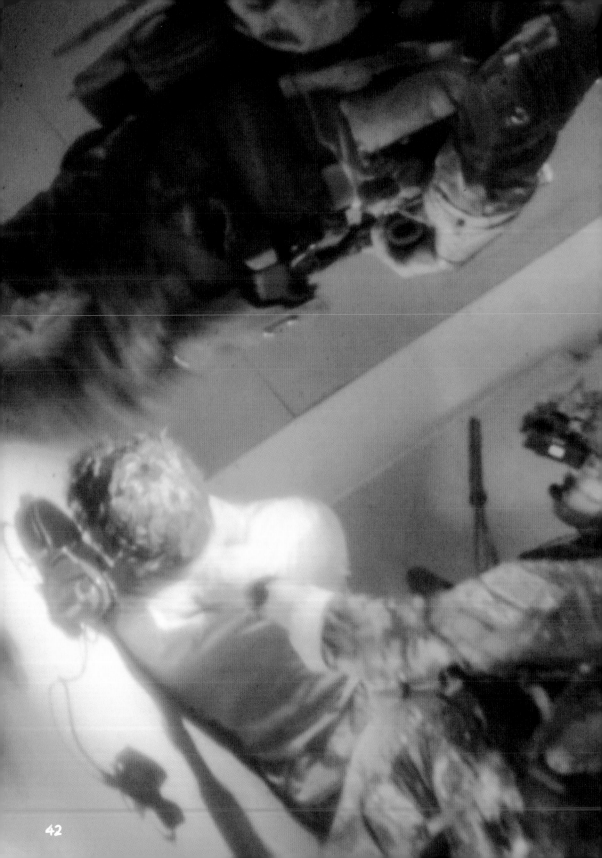

Green Berets try to stop **terrorists** before they can strike. They work with United States **allies** in foreign countries to hunt down violent international criminals and bring them to justice. They also disrupt terrorist information networks and cut off their money supplies.

Green Beret team members practice capturing a criminal.

CHAPTER 12

THE FUTURE

Special Forces soldiers call themselves the quiet professionals. Their success stories remain largely untold. But modern warfare often depends on **covert**, small-unit missions instead of large-scale battles. The Green Berets are well-trained for these tough assignments.

Whatever future challenges await, the Green Berets are ready to meet them head-on.

XTREME
CHALLENGE

TAKE THE QUIZ BELOW AND
PUT WHAT YOU'VE LEARNED TO THE TEST!

1) Green Berets are part of what US military branch?

2) What is the Green Berets' motto?

3) How did these Special Forces members get the name Green Berets?

4) What is a rebreather? Why do Special Forces swimmers like it?

5) What is an "A-Team"?

6) What are some of the important missions that Green Berets perform?

7) What is "fast roping"?

8) What nickname do Special Forces soldiers call themselves? Why?

GLOSSARY

allies – Nations or groups that fight together against a common enemy.

assault rifle – The most commonly used weapon used by today's armed forces. They are fired from the shoulder in either semiautomatic mode (one shot or short burst every time the trigger is pulled), or in fully automatic mode (the weapon fires rapidly until the trigger is released or ammo runs out).

commando – Highly trained soldiers who specialize in raids, sometimes using techniques such as rappelling or parachuting to reach their targets. Commandos often use stealth to attack the enemy. They are also sometimes used to rescue hostages.

covert – Something that is secret or not openly admitted.

exfiltrate – To secretly withdraw troops from a dangerous area, often from behind enemy lines.

guerrilla warfare – Small groups of fighters who raid or sabotage larger armed forces. They surprise and confuse the enemy.

insurgent forces – Rebellious armed forces who try to topple governments. Insurgent forces often use unconventional warfare tactics such as terrorism.

stealth – The ability to avoid detection.

terrorist – A person who uses violence and fear to gain an advantage politically or for religious purposes. Counterterrorism is measures designed to combat or prevent terrorists.

War on Terror – An international effort, led by the United States and the United Kingdom, to eliminate terrorist groups such as al-Qaeda in countries including Afghanistan, Philippines, and Iraq.

ONLINE RESOURCES

Booklinks
NONFICTION NETWORK
FREE! ONLINE NONFICTION RESOURCES

To learn more about Green Berets, please visit **abdobooklinks.com** or scan this QR code. These links are routinely monitored and updated to provide the most current information available.

INDEX